GW00471824

The White Horses

The White Horses are a feature of the Wi
suited to hill figures having steep chalk sca
old, the oldest in Wiltshire being cut in 17
in Oxfordshire is the prehistoric Uffington \
thirteen but only eight are visible today in varying states of splendour.

The horses visible today, in order of age, are:

Westbury White Horse, **Cherhill** White Horse, **Pewsey** White Horse, **Marlborough** White Horse, **Alton Barnes** White Horse, **Hackpen Hill** White Horse, **Broad Town** White Horse and **Devizes** White Horse.

The 'lost' five have become overgrown though their approximate position is known. They were:

Devizes old horse cut in 1845 by local shoemakers and hence known as Snob's Horse, snob being a dialect word for shoemaker. It was just below Oliver's Castle.

Ham Hill or **Inkpen** horse is now totally lost but was cut in the 1860s or 1870s by Mr Wright on a steep slope on Ham Hill near Inkpen Beacon five miles south of Hungerford.

Pewsey old horse was cut by Robert Pile about 1785 on Pewsey Hill, close to the site of the new horse.

Rockley horse on Rockley Down was discovered by ploughing in 1948 but has now completely disappeared due to subsequent ploughing.

Tan Hill horse, or possibly donkey, was only referred to in one book, Wiltshire Folklore by Kathleen Wiltshire published in 1975. In 2002 the webmaster of the excellent Wiltshire White Horses website wiltshirewhitehorses.org.uk found the location.

Maps

Maps in this book are reproduced by permission of Ordnance Survey on behalf of The Controller of Her Majesty's Stationery Office © Crown copyright. Licence No.100033886

The Walks' Authors

These walks were originally created by Catharine Sharples, Sue Melvin and Tim Lewis, who wish to thank other members of the Mid-Wilts Group of Ramblers who have assisted in many ways.

© published by Mid-Wilts Ramblers, 2021
Printed in England by Corsham Print
Unit 4, Leafield Way, Leafield Industrial Estate, Corsham, SN13 9SW
Tel. 01225 812 930, www.corshamprint.co.uk

Contents

The abbreviations for named walks are explained on page 30.

Alton Barnes Horse

Distance: 7 miles or a shorter walk 4 miles

Explorer Map: 157   **Grid Ref.:** SU115637

Start: Knap Hill (Pewsey Downs or Walkers Hill) car park

What3Words: foil.rents.proved   **Nearest Post Code:** SN8 4JX

Mainly a downland walk with excellent views and close to the white horse.

From the car park **[1]** cross the road, go through the gate and then immediately left through the next gate, following the MWW waymarks. Head diagonally left uphill towards the 'pointed' hill – Walkers Hill, with Adam's Grave, a long barrow, at its summit. Through two more gates and on up, always heading towards Adam's Grave until you come to a low bank and depression. Bear right along the earthwork and you will shortly see a path on your left leading to the top of Adam's Grave **[2]**. *There is a fine view from the top.*

Retrace your steps down Adam's Grave, leaving the MWW but joining the WHT, and keep following a path straight ahead and then curving slightly left into a shallow valley and then up over the left shoulder of the hill.

Watch out for an excellent view of the White Horse as the path bends round to the right. The path goes above the top of the horse **[3]** which is fenced off. *It was rechalked in 2019 helped by the army dropping bags of chalk from a Chinook helicopter, and the chalk was spread by local people.* Continue ahead and glance back as you reach the high point of the shoulder for a last glimpse of the horse. The path becomes rather indistinct but keep following the contour of the hill, staying on the same level and curving round to the right.

At a water trough **[4]** bear right again following the contours to stay level and go through a gate marked WHT and MWW. Follow the head of a valley or coombe which drops steeply to the left, keeping the fence on your right and going through another gate.

Continue until you see a gate on the right marked WHT and MWW turning away from the head of the combe **[5]**. Go through this gate and keep the fence on your right.

On your left you can see the banks of the Wansdyke coming in from the left and Silbury Hill ahead. When you reach a gate marked WHT and MWW and a track, cross the track and go over the stile on the other side.

Turn immediately right **[6]** onto the bank of the Wansdyke to join the WP. *This is a very impressive section of the Wansdyke.* At a dip in the path, ignore the stile on the right and continue on the Wansdyke enjoying the views but also watching out for holes in the path.

At a major break in the bank, head down to the path at the bottom and go through a field gate **[7]**. Continue along the track with the bank on your

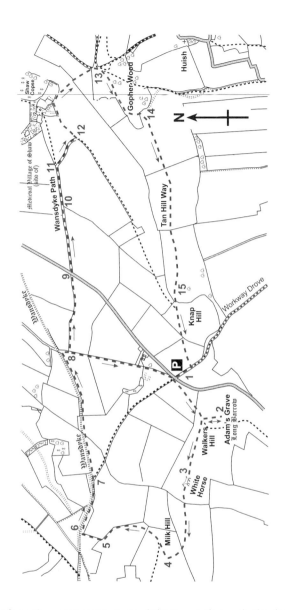

right. Just before the next gate, turn right to go through the bank, then turn left to walk along the edge of the field with the Wansdyke bank on your left. At the next fence you can either go through the small gate then continue with the bank on your left or you can scramble up to the top of the bank and walk along the top. At the next fence you will need to rejoin the path at the foot of the bank. Now walk between the bank on your left and a fence on your right as the Wansdyke is very overgrown here. As you approach a track, bear half right to meet it, away from the Wansdyke.

At the junction **[8]** with the track you have a choice:

For a shorter walk, turn right and head down a track towards farm buildings, through three gates (two with stiles) and back to the road and the car park **[1]**.

For a longer walk go straight over the track and over the stile marked WP. Continue ahead on a grassy track aiming for a large beech tree which is in a hollow. *On your left is a very overgrown part of the Wansdyke marked by dense trees and bushes.* Pass to the right of the large beech tree and continue down to the road with the fence on your left.

Cross the road **[9]** and through the gate marked WP and follow the track uphill with the fence on your left. The track meanders a little but towards the top of the hill you will see a gate marked WP.

Go through this onto a path **[10]** with hedges on both sides. If this path is overgrown you may need to walk in the field next to it. Follow this until you come to the corner of a field to your left. The WP goes off to the left **[11]** but you need to bear right between hedges/trees and a fence.

At a junction **[12]** turn left along the edge of a field with the fence on your right and follow this fence to the edge of a wood. Ignore a small path leading off to the left. Continue with the wood on your left and the fence on your right as the path curves right and then downhill. At the bottom you will see the path climbing the hill in front of you between two fences and lots of vegetation. At the top you come out between two metal field gates both marked 'Private Farm Land No Public Right of Way'. Continue straight ahead along a short section between wire fences and then straight across a field to trees.

Go through the gate and turn right for 30 yards, where you come to a major junction **[13]** of paths and tracks. Go through the small 'walkers' gate on your right, thus re-joining the MWW and walk uphill, with Gopher Woods on your left, to a field gate and stile marked MWW. Go through this and keep straight on to the top of the hill and through another gate and stile in the top left hand corner of the field. Go half left towards the left-hand tree ahead, in front of which can soon be seen a tall signpost **[14]**.

Turn right and walk along the ridge with extensive views towards Salisbury Plain on your left. Go through a squeeze stile marked MWW and Public Footpath, not the small gate to the right of this. Continue along the ridge with the fence on your right. As you progress, Adam's Grave comes into view briefly. Go through another gate/stile marked MWW.

At the brow of the hill **[15]** you will see Adam's Grave again and, to the right of that, the car park. Continue down the hill through two more gates/stiles and turn right at the bottom to the car park **[1]**.

Broad Town Horse

Distance: 8 miles

Explorer Map: 157   **Grid Ref.:** SU090778

Start: layby

What3Words: jump.festivity.crafts   **Post Code:** SN4 7RG

An interesting walk through woods, an Iron Age hill fort (Bincknoll Castle), villages and farmland with tantalising glimpses of two White Horses.

The route begins at the southern end of Broad Town, where the main road intersects with Pye Lane and Chapel Lane **[1]**. Go down Pye Lane and follow the lane past the last of the houses and between fields until you reach a sharp right hand bend and Springfield Villa **[2]**. Turn left up the tarmac lane and just before the lane bends to the right, with a thatched cottage high up on your right, turn left up a footpath by a yellow road grit bin **[3]**. Go up this path. At a fork, just past the footpath markings on a post, ignore the footpath straight ahead and bear right uphill **[4]** until you come to the crest of the escarpment. Turn left along the escarpment looking out for good views of the Broad Town White Horse on the slope. At the first field boundary on your right **[5]**, turn right to follow the field boundary, with the boundary on your right, until you meet a road **[6]**.

Cross the road and go over the stile almost opposite. The path goes straight across this field aiming for a small gap in the trees on the far side but it is often easier to turn right and follow the field boundary around the field. Go through the gap and again, although the path goes straight across, it is easier to turn left and follow the field boundary round, with views of the Hackpen White Horse in the distance, until you see a metal gate which leads out onto a track (Vize Lane) **[7]**. Turn left and follow the wide gravel track to a road at a sharp bend on the edge of the village of Broad Hinton **[8]**.

Turn right and go up the tarmac lane (not the main road) which leads to some large houses and soon becomes gravel and then a wide grassy curving track. Soon you may glimpse a church on your left through the trees. Turn left at a footpath crossroads **[9]**, bearing slightly left onto a path that runs alongside the churchyard and go through the gravel and grassed area (the church car park). Turn left along the road for a short distance until you come to a grassy triangle with a well. Turn right here onto the main road and shortly after turn left into Post Office Lane **[10]**. Look for a footpath sign indicating left into what appears to be the drive to a house (Cotsmoor House). Take the left of the two drives and very soon you will come to a 'crossroads' of two narrow tarmac fenced-in paths with metal barriers. Take the right hand of these and walk along it until you reach a stile on the right. Go over this and turn left to follow the edge of the field and over another stile.

Head diagonally across the field, passing to the right of some gnarled

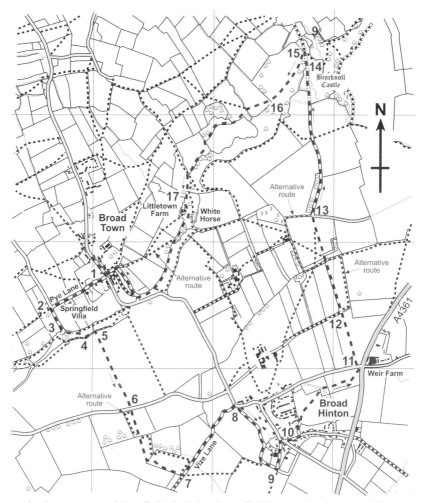

trees in the centre of the field (originally a field boundary), to a stile onto a track. Go over this and over a second stile on the other side of the track. Continue in the same direction passing an electricity pole in the middle of the field and aiming for a stile in the far left corner of this field by a white house, which is by the crossroads with the A4361 Avebury-Swindon road and near Weir Farm **[11]**. Go over the stile and the footbridge and cross the minor road. Turn left and almost immediately right to follow a long straight grassy bridleway between two fields. At the top of the slope go through the metal field gate **[12]**.

Once again the path goes straight across the field but it is easier to turn right and follow the field boundary around three sides to a metal gate on the right. Go through this, again the path goes straight across but it is easier to turn left along one side of the field boundary to a gravel track. Turn right and follow this past a copse on the left and a building. The track bends right and then left. Follow it **[13]** alongside a small wood on your left. Continue along the track past the end of the wood and at a path junction keep straight on, ignoring the clearly marked footpath/track to the left. Here the route becomes a rough grass track, continuing towards a low mound which is part of the ramparts of Bincknoll Castle **[14]**. Walk into the central area of the Iron Age Fort; this is a lovely spot for a picnic or drinks break.

To leave Bincknoll Castle continue in the same direction as before down a wide steep track. Where the trees open out, look for a metal field gate and stile on your left **[15]**. Go through this. The path becomes a little indistinct but keep parallel to the left hand field edge, alongside the wooded escarpment, dropping down to a stile at the end of the field. Go over the stile and through a narrow strip of cultivated land, often maize. If this looks impassable, turn up hill to go around the top of the maize and then back down a track to the end of the wood. Both routes bring you to a track **[16]**. Leave this track by a large tree (almost opposite where the path emerges from the maize) to follow a fairly indistinct path through a field, keeping the woods and escarpment on your left and crossing a small stream at the far end. Continue in the same general direction through fields, over a stile and into a very overgrown field. Follow the winding path through here and through a walkers' gate. Ignore the gate on the left temptingly labelled Public Footpath (this is the far end of the original official route, however this path is no longer safe due to a landslip) and continue in the same general direction keeping the wood and the escarpment on your left. Continue across this field, through another gate way. Just before you reach Little Town Farmhouse, by a dilapidated rusty corrugated-iron building **[17]**, look up to your left and you will see the Broad Town White Horse on the slope above. Shortly after you will reach the rear of Little Town Farmhouse.

Keep left of the farmhouse and follow the often muddy path past a white cottage on your left. *You can take a short cut a little way past the cottage as the next stile/gate comes into view, by going over a stile on the right and walking diagonally left across the field to a track with a cattle grid. Look back here for a view of the White Horse. Turn left and follow the track to the junction with Horns Lane. Keep straight on to the main road and to where you parked [1]*. Alternatively keep straight on and go over the stile and then follow the track though the trees with a fence on your right. This eventually leads you to a gate into a tarmac lane with houses! Turn down the lane (Horns Lane) and at the bottom turn left into Chapel Lane. This leads you out onto the main road, turn right onto Broad Town Road, to where you parked **[1]**.

Cherhill White Horse

Distance: 7 or 9 miles; for a shorter 3½ mile walk see page 9

Explorer Map: 157   **Grid Ref.:** SU020671

Start: Car park at Smallgrain Picnic Area

What3Words: noise.apricot.earphones   **Post Code:** SN10 2LP

Both options include downland walking with wide views and a Bronze Age, later Iron Age, hillfort as well as good views of the horse. The main walk includes some woodland, a village and a Nature Reserve.

Longer walk.

From Smallgrain Picnic Area car park **[1]**, go up the slope at the far end of the car park and follow the path up and then down some steps onto the byway and turn right. Stay on the byway until you reach the Wildlife Trust's information panel for Morgan's Hill **[2]** on the right.

Opposite the information panel, go through two gates onto the bridleway and proceed downhill and straight ahead through a field gate. Stay on this path until you arrive at a third field gate leading onto a track. Turn right and follow the track until you reach a junction. Turn left here and continue until you see the waymarked field gate on your right just as the track bends sharp left. Go through the gate and then turn left through the next field gate.

Once through this gate, bear right and go downhill with the church of St Mary's **[3]** on your right. Just past the church you will notice a stile on your right. Cross this onto the gravel track, turn left and continue down the embanked track until you come to a T-junction.

Turn right here and continue along the road, past a 'No Through Road' sign and then past a gate on the right marked 'Private Road to South Farm & Toghill'. Where the bridleways fork take the right hand fork marked South Farm. Continue along the track until you are leaving the wooded area where you will see a gate on your right with a waymarker pointing to the left **[4]**. The path you must follow is on the other (left) side of the track and goes downhill just before the bend. At the bottom, go over the stile or through the gate and turn right. *Ahead of you, on the horizon is Oldbury Castle Hillfort and Lansdowne/Cherhill Monument.*

Follow the field edge with the fence on the right, you will see a National Trust sign 'Calstone Coombes' with an adjacent kissing gate. Go through this and proceed straight ahead with the fence on your right and on through two gates or gateways. Follow the bottom of the valley of Ranscombe Bottom until it bends sharp left **[5]**. Go straight on up a steep sided valley* with coarse tussock grass to a stile at the top. From here, look straight ahead and walk towards a gap, once a stile, in the fence with the Monument on your left. When you meet the track turn left. **[6]** *(If you wish to return to the car park without seeing the horse, turn right at this point and walk down to the Roman*

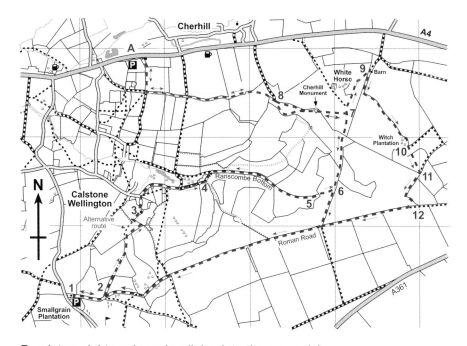

Road, turn right again and walk back to the car park.)

* If you miss this path and walk too far up the coombe, simply climb to the top and follow the fence round to the right until you reach the stile.

To continue to the monument and White Horse follow the path straight up the hill. Just past a copse on the right, keep right and the track becomes much narrower. Go through the gate into Cherhill Down and Oldbury Castle Hillfort National Trust reserve and you will see the top of the Monument coming into view. Continue straight on and through a field gate waymarked WHT and WR. Continue straight on with the Monument on your left until a faint track on the left **[7]** takes you into the hillfort through the double banks of the 'main entrance' to the hillfort.

As you walk towards the Monument, to your left you can see the masts on Morgan's Hill and look down on Ranscombe Bottom where you were earlier.

Take the track to the left of the Monument and head downhill on a clearly defined track. Ignore a grassy path which veers off to the right, you will come back along this. Go through a field gate and follow the track which skirts a knoll on your right. You will pass a field gate on your left and then see two field gates on your right. Go through the second gate and then turn sharp right by the information panel and through a kissing gate **[8]**. Follow this track up towards the monument enjoying excellent views of the White Horse.

As you near the Monument you will join the track you took earlier. Retrace your steps back to the Monument. Continuing in the same general direction,

8

take the left of the two grassy tracks leading away from the Monument, through the ramparts again and you will meet the track you were on previously **[7]**.

You now have a choice.

To shorten this walk you can turn right and follow the track down to the Roman Road (now a wide track) and turn right again to follow the Roman Road back to the car park.

To do the Witch Plantation Loop walk, turn left and follow the track down to a barn **[9]**. At the barn turn sharp right (almost back on yourself) to take the track marked BYWAY leading downhill away from the barn. This track is partly surfaced with tarmac chippings but can be very rutted and muddy in several places. Follow the track which bends sharp left, *giving fine views of the Marlborough Downs and Silbury Hill*, until you have passed a small copse (Witch Plantation) on your right **[10]**. Leave the track where it bends sharp left, by taking a NT stile ahead and on your right. There is no obvious path here so head half left up and over the hill aiming for the top left hand corner and a stile which leads on to a track **[11]**. Turn right onto the track and follow it downhill, looking down on the A361 and the nearer Roman Road which you join **[12]**. Turn right and follow the track back to the car park.

Shorter walk:

Distance: 3½ miles

Explorer Map: 157   **Grid Ref.:** SU026698

Start: Large layby on the south side of the A4 at Quemerford Gate **[A]**

What3Words: examine.universally.attic   **Post Code:** SN11 8UN

Walk to the eastern end of the layby **[A]** (away from Calne) and walk along the grass verge to a track on the right beside a house and a footpath post sign 'The Downs, Calstone'. Follow the track over the cattle grid, past farm buildings and through a gate. Continue straight ahead through two fields (the first is sometimes a small campsite).

At the footpath/bridleway junction take the broad bridleway to the left. Follow this bridleway as it climbs steadily up hill. At the derelict building with a bridleway crossing continue straight ahead on the footpath (can be muddy/slippery when wet). Climbing steadily for some distance, continue through a gate with the National Trust sign 'Cherhill Down, Oldbury Castle'. Continue straight on uphill toward the Lansdowne (Cherhill) Monument and go left around a low knoll (with very sparse, windblown trees) down to two gates. Go through the first gate; turn sharp right and continue through the second, kissing gate **[8]** by the information panel. Follow this track up toward the Monument *enjoying excellent views of the Cherhill White Horse and the Monument.*

To return, simply retrace your steps.

Devizes White Horse

Distance: 7 or 8 miles and shorter walks from 1 to 4 miles

Explorer Maps: 157   **Grid Ref.**: SU003617

Start: Wharf car park

What3Words: dock.galloping.smart   **Post Code:** SN10 1EA

There are other start points detailed at the end.

The walk begins in the town, along the canal then up to the White Horse, through woods and to Oliver's Castle with many outstanding views. The return is in open downland and fields back down to the town.

From the car park **[1]** take the towpath heading east with the canal on your left. You will pass under London Road at bridge 138 and will then have views of the back gardens of the properties along that road.

On arriving at bridge 136 (Coate bridge **[2]** which has a plaque on it stating that it was rebuilt in 1990), go under it but immediately turn sharp right off the towpath and up steps to arrive at the tarmac road you have just gone under (Windsor Drive). Turn right over the bridge and proceed to the main road (A361). Cross over to the opposite pavement and turn right.

Shortly before the roundabout look for a signposted footpath to the left **[3]** with hedges on either side. Follow this into a small car park. Here look for a narrow path between a hedge on the left and a fence on the right and follow this into what appears to be a garden and then out onto Folly Road. (If this path is very overgrown bear half left through the car park and climb through a two wooden-rail fence into what appears to be a garden and out onto Folly Road.) Turn right and follow this road, with fleeting good views of the horse, for about half a mile to the sign for Roundway village.

Walk through the village, turning right in front of the phone box **[4]** *(now a book store)*. Follow the road and at the last of the cottages look for a Natural England permissive footpath to enter the field on your right. Turn left and walk up the hill, along the field edge, separated from the road by the hedge.

Exit the field through a gap **[5]** near a field gate and turn right uphill on the road.

There's a car parking area here **[6]** and below it is the entrance to the field with the white horse. After spending time in the horse's field, if desired, return to the road, cross it, then turn left to enter and walk through Leipzig Plantation.

Exit at the squeeze stile **[7]** and continue straight on, until you reach a further parking area. Cross the road where the tarmac comes to an end and go through a gate **[8]** and across the field into Roundway Hill Covert.

Follow the footpath through the woods, initially just inside the wood next to the field on your right. As the path bends to the right **[9]** follow a path to

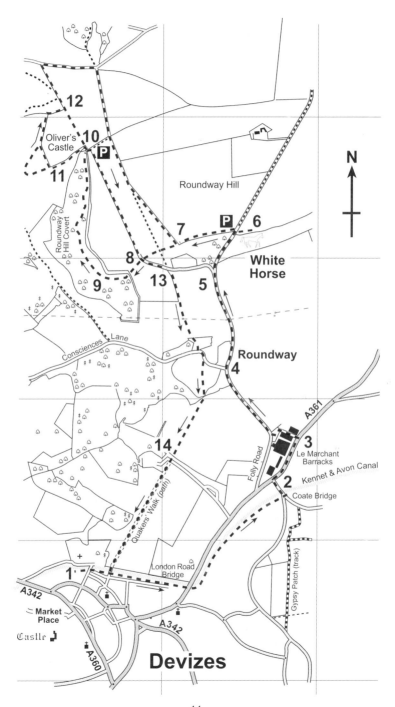

N

12

Oliver's Castle 10

11

Roundway Hill

Roundway Hill Covert

7

6

White Horse

8

9

13

5

Consciences Lane

Roundway

4

A361

14

3
Le Marchant Barracks

Folly Road

2

Kennet & Avon Canal

Coate Bridge

Quakers' Walk (path)

Gypsy Patch (track)

London Road Bridge

1

A342

Market Place

Castle

A342

A360

Devizes

the left towards the lower side of the wood but do not go down the very steep slope. As you leave the first 'lookout', go down steps to the left and follow a route in and out through the woods enjoying the occasional fantastic views to the west over Rowde and Bromham and later to the north towards Olivor'o Castle. Eventually, the route bears right up the remains of wooden steps to a path, turn left here.

Exit the woods into another parking area **[10]**, turn left and then left again through a gate marked Private but you are allowed to use it. This leads to Oliver's Castle, an Iron Age hill fort.

Continue along the footpath with a deep wooded coombe on the left **[11]**. *You can explore the whole of the hill fort and admire the views which stretch for miles. It's a great picnic spot and look out for butterflies and wild orchids. The coombes were formed at the end of the Ice Age by meltwater from the glaciers gouging out valleys in the permafrost.*

Continue around Oliver's Castle past a tall wooden post and then an English Nature information board. Through a kissing gate and then a walkers gate to exit at the far (north) end **[12]**.

Here you have a choice.

For a longer walk turn left and continue to the T-junction and then turn right. After about 600 yards turn right again onto a degraded tarmac track to rejoin the WR. When the track turns right, continue ahead along the edge of a large field, with the fence on the left. On reaching the wood ahead, Leipzig Plantation, follow the path round to the right, then veer left across two deeply rutted tracks and turn right along a third, smoother one to the car park at **[8]**. Turn left down the road to **[13]**.

For a shorter walk turn right and follow the track (the MWW) back to **[10]**, past the parking area, through another parking area **[8]**. Turn left and follow the now tarmac road down to **[13]**.

Both walks

On the right hand side of the road, go through a V stile by galvanised gates **[13]**. Walk downhill with the hedge to your right, passing the pylon. At the bottom of the field, go through a kissing gate, a copse then another kissing gate, onto a road.

Turn left, follow the road which bends sharp right, to reach a set of shallow steps which go into a field on the right. Turn left along the edge of the field, with a hedge to the left, then pass between fields to a gap in the hedge next to a house. Turn slightly right onto a broad straight gravel path which soon becomes a narrower stony path between hedges.

Cross over a tarmac road **[14]** which leads to Roundway House to the right and continue straight on along a grassy path onto Quakers' Walk and continue to the end where you'll see large gates. Go through these, over the canal bridge and turn right along the canal towpath to the car park **[1]**.

Shorter walks

Drive up and park at any of the following and pick up the route

    a) After leaving Roundway village fork right, go up the hill and park at the White Horse **[6]**.

    b) After leaving Roundway village fork left and go up the hill to the parking area at the end of the tarmac road **[8]**.

    c) After leaving Roundway village fork left, past the parking area at **[8]** and continue along the gravel track to another parking area near Oliver's Castle **[10]**.

Roundway Down

View from Morgan's Hill

13

Westbury White Horse

This is the oldest White Horse in Wiltshire, dating back to 1778. The present figure was preceded by a much older version at the same site, the date and origin of which are unknown. Legend has it that it was cut as a memorial to one of King Alfred's victories over the Danes at the battle of Ethandun in 878 AD.

Cherhill White Horse

This horse was cut under the direction of Dr Alsop of Calne, also known as the "mad doctor", who shouted instructions over a megaphone from the main road in 1780. It is situated under an ancient earthwork called Oldbury Castle. Its eye (four feet across) was once filled with upturned bottles which sparkled in the sunlight but were at the mercy of souvenir hunters.

Pewsey White Horse

The original horse was cut in 1785, and reputedly featured a rider. It was re-designed in 1937 by Mr George Marples and cut by the Pewsey Fire Brigade to celebrate the coronation of King George VI.

Marlborough White Horse

This is Wiltshire's smallest white horse and was designed in 1804 by William Canning, a pupil at Mr Greasley's Academy in Marlborough, and cut into Granham hill above the River Kennet by the boys of Greasley's Academy, not Marlborough College.

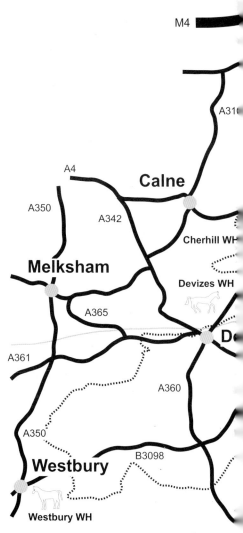

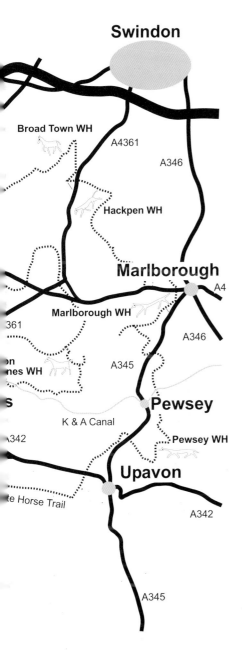

Alton Barnes White Horse

It was cut in 1812 at the expense of the landowner, Mr Robert Pile of Manor Farm. His first contractor fled with an advance payment of £20 after drawing a sketch of the horse. The contractor was eventually found and hanged for a list of crimes. In 2010 the horse underwent a major renovation, overseen by landowner Tim Carson and the Alton Barnes Parish Council, when 150 tons of fresh chalk were delivered to the site by helicopter, which volunteers then used to replenish the surface of the figure. It was refreshed again in 2019.

Hackpen Hill White Horse

The horse was cut in 1837 by the Parish Clerk of Broad Hinton to commemorate the coronation of Queen Victoria.

Broad Town White Horse

This is a small white horse which was cut in 1863 but was lost until the 1990s. The horse is regularly scoured by the Broad Town White Horse Restoration Society, which was formed in 1991.

Devizes White Horse

This was a new white horse for the millennium. The Devizes White Horse faces to the right, while all the others face to the left, it looks as if it is going from Devizes to meet the Alton Barnes White Horse. It was designed by Peter Greed, a former pupil of Devizes Grammar School and cut in 1999 by some 200 local people with the assistance of heavy machinery supplied by Pearce Civil Engineering.

15

Hackpen White Horse

Distance: 9 miles and a shorter walk of 4½ miles

Explorer Maps: 157   **Grid Ref**.: SU129747

Start: Hackpen Hill car park

What3Words: plenty.tribe.bleak   **Nearest Post Code:** SN4 9NR

There are two options, a shorter and a longer walk, both starting from Hackpen Hill Car Park. The start of both is very open and can be bleak but later they are pleasant walks along tracks, through fields and small woods. The longer walk includes the hillfort of Barbury Castle.

Longer walk 9 miles

Walk north-east away from the road from the Hackpen Hill car park **[1]** along the Ridgeway, towards Barbury Castle. Pass three clumps of trees on your left which were planted in the Victorian age. *After the last one, as the track descends, there is a good view of Barbury Castle half right.* The track descends gently and veers right to arrive at a road **[2]**.

Turn right for 30 yards, then through a gate on your left uphill to continue on the Ridgeway. Walk through the ramparts of Barbury Castle **[3]**, which is an Iron Age hill fort. As you leave the fort, go through a gate and keeping the fence/hedge on your right go through another gate to the car park (with toilets) **[4]** on your left. As the road bends left, continue on the path near the hedge on your right to arrive at a bridle gate onto a road.

Turn right, it changes from tarmac to gravel, and after about 120 yards continue straight ahead when the Ridgeway bears left into a field. *From here there are good views across Smeathe's Ridge and The Ridgeway on your left.* Soon after the track bends right, you pass Four Mile Clump **[5]** on your left. *'Four Mile' in the name gives a hint that this is in fact the old Marlborough to Swindon turnpike road, the clump being four miles from the centre of Marlborough.* Continue ever onwards. Ignore another byway going off to the left by a grassy/muddy triangle.

Follow this track which bends slightly right and later, as it starts to descend more steeply and bear left, turn right through a metal field gate into an area used to store stable manure. Go straight past and exit through a bridle gate. Walk half left across a gently sloping field to the left hand corner of a fenced off lower field and through a bridle gate. Descend steeply to a road where there is an old stone milepost in the green triangle opposite, showing the distance to London as 77 miles.

Cross the road **[6]** and go along the road opposite into the tiny village of Rockley. Pass All Saints church on your left, then the village pond on your right. Pass a large stables on your left and at the end of the village **[7]**, turn right along a signposted byway. Soon after, turn left along the same byway along the right-hand edge of a large field. Continue through a second

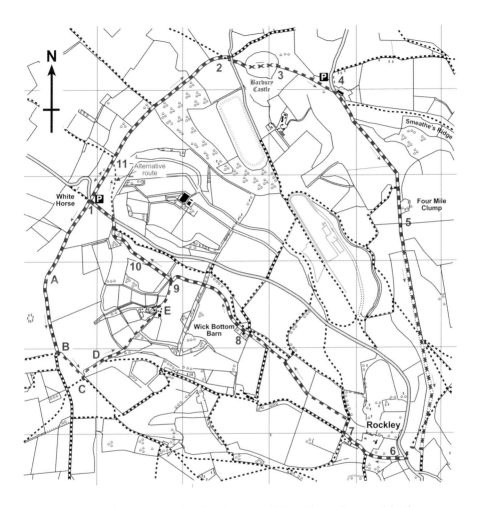

large field to arrive at a road. Continue walking along the road in the same direction until you reach a crucifixion shrine.

Go straight on past Wick Bottom Barn **[8]**, to the left of the shrine. The road curves gently to the right and then to the left and passes through a thin strip of beech and box woodland. Just after the road bends more sharply left and ascends, turn right onto an unsurfaced track, signposted 'To the Ridgeway' **[9]**. This track follows the bottom of a valley for some way, then begins to climb as it passes a picket gate with an arch of roses and then Fortnight **[10]** on the left, with its sign saying 'Slow, Toads on Track'. It passes through a wooded area, getting gradually steeper, and as it levels out it arrives at a road. Turn left and walk along the right hand verge of the road for a short distance back to the Hackpen Hill car park **[1]**.

(If you prefer to avoid walking along the road, go straight across it and follow the track with the hedge on your right. At the dip, do not go through the double metal field gates, but take the path up out of the dip which passes to the left of the hedge. Follow this until you meet the Ridgeway **[11]**. Turn left along the Ridgeway and walk back to the car park).

Shorter Walk - 4½ miles

Cross the road carefully.

To your right you will see a metal kissing gate, this goes down to the White Horse which you can touch but please don't walk on it.

Walk along the track (TR), into the dip, ignore a byway to the right **[A]**, continue up the hill and it then levels out. You will reach a signpost and an information board about the Berwick Bassett Dewpond. At the signpost turn left onto a bridleway, leaving the Ridgeway **[B]**.

Walk between the two hedges, ignore a path crossing and continue until you come to another track. Ahead of you in the bushes is the intriguingly named Glory Ann **[C]**, *possibly an old clay pit or dew pond but not visible or marked on most maps today*. Turn left and follow the field boundary round to

the right then to the left, ignoring a gate on the right. Continue on the level until you come to a fork **[D]** and take the left fork which keeps fairly level along the side of the valley. Ignore a track to the left and continue with a small wood on your right. When you reach a gate go through and go downhill towards Wick Down Farm **[E]**.

Go through the farm yard with a 'horse walker' and a stone and slate barn on the right. At a junction with two gravel tracks, follow the surfaced road round to the right then left up a gentle hill and then downhill. Where the road bends right near the bottom, turn left along a gravel track and follow the route for the longer walk from **[9]**.

*Old Signpost
near Rockley*

18

Marlborough White Horse

Distance: 5½ miles

Explorer Maps: 157   **Grid Ref.:** SU162666

Start: Clatford Bottom car park in West Woods

What3Words: critic.pronouns.leans   **Nearest Post Code:** SN8 4DZ

A view of the least known horse with a walk through woods, over downland and either through a pretty village or through an uncultivated valley bottom.

From the car park **[1]** walk back down the track, cross the road and go over the stile opposite **[2]**. Go diagonally up the field to a stile in the left hand corner **[3]**. Go over the stile and continue walking along the top of the hill with the hedge on your right. Continue alongside the hedge until there is a stile through a gap in the hedge **[4]**. Go over this stile and into a large field.

Follow the edge of the field with the hedge on your left. As the ground starts to go gently downhill **[5]** follow a track half right across the field, keeping a small copse of trees and bushes to your left, to the end of the tall hedge on your right **[6]**. Then turn right and immediately left to take a path between hedges.

This leads out on a tarmac road, Manton Drove **[7]**. Go left down this for about 100 yards, then turn right **[8]** (waymarked WHT and WP) onto a strip between two fields. On reaching the far edge, go left, with the hedge to your right, and step over the logged stile into the next field. *You will now see parts of the town of Marlborough in front of you.* Go half left down this field aiming for a stile half way down the other side. Go over this stile, pass through a strip of woodland, and go over a second stile. This takes you into a long field **[9]**, stay on the crest of the hill with the hedge on your right. *You can see Marlborough College Chapel with its huge steep roof and tall slim spire to your half left, and further left the tower of St George's Church Preshute.* After passing through a small beech wood *(part of Marlborough College Nature Trail)*, go left **[10]** alongside a sunken track.

The path descends in a sweeping right hand curve then veers off to the left near the bottom to pass through a gap in the trees into the field below.

Keep the field edge to your left and go through a metal kissing gate at the end into a path between fences **[11]**. Continue down the path and through a small car park to the left of the tennis courts to arrive at Preshute House **[12]** near the car park for St George's church. To see the very pretty church walk a little further down the lane into the churchyard **[13]**.

To see the Marlborough White Horse, take the wide, stony track between the car park of St George's church and the tennis courts (tennis courts on your right), in the direction of Marlborough. Just as you arrive at the second set of tennis courts, the White Horse can be seen half right on the hill behind them **[14]**. It may be very green!

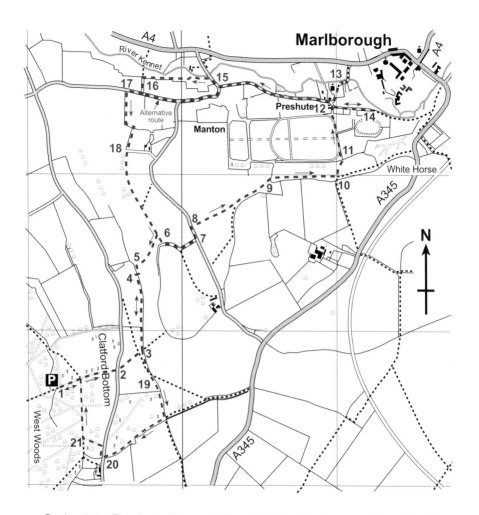

Go back to Preshute House **[12]** and follow the lane westwards with a high wall on the left and buildings (Preshute House) on the right. Walk along this mainly tree lined lane to the village of Manton, passing Manton Grange on your left.

At the T-junction **[15]** you have a choice, **but beware**, the first option may be badly overgrown in summer, and flooded in winter.

Option 1:

If you are feeling adventurous and the weather has been fairly dry, turn right, pass the Oddfellows pub on your left and just before the bridge over the river turn left into the play park of Manton Jubilee Field. In the far right hand corner there is a metal gate leading onto a wooden bridge over the river. Cross this and follow the path through trees *(there are glimpses of the river and sluice gates of Manton Mill)* as it turns left to another wooden bridge back over the river. The path goes straight on to another stile. Cross this and turn right to go through two more possibly overgrown or flooded areas behind some houses. At the far end in the left hand corner there is a stile. Cross this and turn left between two fences up to the road **[16]**. Turn right along the road away from the village.

Option 2:

Turn left at the T-junction and continue through the pretty village of Manton with several thatched cottages, a phone box book store and Preshute School's "rainwall". You will pass Manton Drove on your left.

Both routes:

Just after you leave the village you will see some steps on your left going up a bank and into a field **[17]**. Go up these, over the stile and straight ahead with the hedge on your right. Follow the path and hedge as they curve left to the corner of the field, go over the stile by the wooden cottage, through a few trees and over a second stile. Walk with the hedge on your right to the corner of the field and go over the stile (beware barbed wire), through a few trees and out into a large field **[18]**.

Turn left, then after about 20 yards turn right along the field edge with woods to your right. Follow the field edge ahead until the end of the wood, then continue in the same direction along a track between two fields, to reach **[6]**. Follow the path curving left briefly and then half right, back across the field with the small copse of bushes on your right to **[5]**. At the hedge turn left for a short distance and look for the stile in the hedge on the right at **[4]**. Cross the stile and follow the path close to the hedge on the left to reach the stile, **[3]**. Go over the stile and continue to walk along the top of the field, with the hedge on your left, until you reach a wooden gate in the hedge **[19]**. Go through this and turn immediately right onto a path through woodland. Follow this until you reach a sunken path on the right, the bank is part of the Wansdyke. This leads gently down to a tarmac road **[20]**.

Turn right down the road for a short distance and take the path on your left going uphill to reach the low waymarked post at **[21]**.

Turn right and follow the path, taking the right-hand path at a fork. Continue until this path reaches a wide track. Turn left and follow the track back to the car park **[1]**.

Pewsey White Horse

Distance: 7 miles

Explorer Maps: 130 and 157   **Grid Ref**.: SU162601

Start: Bouverie Hall car park

What3Words: pounces.storybook.pelted   **Post Code:** SN9 5ES

The first part of this walk is along the Pewsey Avon Trail (PAT), as far as the Manningfords where you have an option to take a small detour (just under 1 mile). You then join the White Horse Trail.

Leave Bouverie Hall Car Park **[1]** and turn right onto North Street, ahead of you is King Alfred's statue. Continue along River Street, then turn right along Church Street and past St John the Baptist church to the next bend. When you reach The Crescent (right hand side of road) head into it and turn onto the signed footpath on the left, continuing straight ahead, between houses. This takes you straight on past the end of several private gardens with views on the left towards Pewsey Hill. Continue along the edge of the sports field. The path emerges on a minor road beside a thatched cottage.

Turn left along a minor road and pass Sharcott House **[2]**. At the junction turn right along a 'Quiet Lane' to Manningford, by the red post box in the wall. Ignore the unsigned turning to the left as you follow the road around to the right, followed by a road junction beside a white thatched cottage. Turn left around the cottage and continue, then cross a bridge over the Avon. After passing under electricity cables, walk about 50 yards and look right for a kissing gate in the hedgerow **[3]**.

Here you have two options:

Option 1:

Continue along the road, until you meet the main A345 at **[4]**.

Option 2:

Cross the field, directly towards the little church of Manningford Abbots. Enter the churchyard by a kissing gate, pass the church porch and exit by a kissing gate. Cross the stile marked PAT, aiming for the gate ahead marked WHT. Go through the wood (which is full of horsetail), over three bridges and exit the wooded area by The Mill, pass the property and turn left along the drive. Turn left onto the road and follow it until you reach several thatched houses. Turn left onto the footpath marked PAT and WHT through a gap in the hedge opposite the White House. Go through the kissing gate (which floods after heavy rain), cross the field and exit through another kissing gate – look for two flat wooden planks covering overgrown ditches. Exit by the kissing gate (you will be back in the field you crossed, past the church, earlier) and turn right along the edge of the field with the large house ahead and then to your left. Go through the 2 field gates, turn left by the barn, and

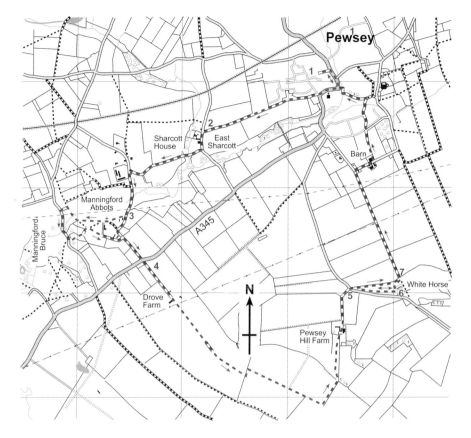

exit the field across a stile and sleeper bridge, turning right onto the road. The road joins the main A345 **[4]**.

Both Routes:

   Cross carefully and join the track to Drove Farm. Remain on the track past some barns, passing under power lines and climb to the brow of the hill keeping the line of trees to the left. As you crest the hill a gate can be seen directly ahead. Pass through the gate and turn immediately left. Proceed around 50 yards and turn right following an obvious track along the bridleway across two fields in a SE direction (exit 1st field by a gate). The bridleway turns left at the fence line at the top of the hill. Near the field corner, a wide, chalky track begins. Go through the gate and continue along the cinder track. When the track passes through a field gate to the right of a wooden fence, keep to the left of the fence to reach a small metal gate into the farmyard of Pewsey Hill Farm. Proceed through the farmyard with the farmhouse to the left and barns on both sides. The track starts to descend. On the bend where the track turns to the right and crosses a cattle grid, go through the gate ahead and follow the original bridleway down the gully to the road.

Turn right, walk 10 yards and cross the road **[5]**. Climb the stile into the field containing the White Horse. Where the path forks take the path on your right and follow the sometimes indistict path as it ascends across access land to reach the White Horse and its enclosure **[6]**. To leave the horse you have a choice of taking the very steep path down **to the left of the enclosure** (WHT) to the kissing gate **[7]** OR retracing your steps, gently downhill, to the fork in the path near **[5]**. From here take the clear path to the right along the bottom of the escarpment keeping the hedge on your left. At the end of the hedge, turn left to the kisssing gate **[7]** *at which point turn back for the best view of the horse.*

Go through the kissing gate and follow the path until reaching the road at a sharp bend. Turn right and after about 200 yards turn left at large barns along the footpath signposted to Pewsey. At Swan Meadow cross the road to a tarmac path between gardens, to a T-junction signposted Kings Corner to the right. Turn left here and follow the footpath, crossing the Avon over a bridge and turning right back onto River Street.

Retrace your steps back to the car park **[1]**.

View over the Vale of Pewsey

24

Westbury White Horse

Distance: 8 miles and two shorter walks of 2½ and 3 miles

Explorer Maps: 143   **Grid Ref.**: ST899513

Start: at the western (Westbury) end of the large car park (Westbury White Horse/Bratton Camp) by three information boards

What3Words: buns.quitter.bagels   **Nearest Post Code:** BA13 4SP

All three walks take you close to the white horse and have far reaching views. The longer walk also gives you excellent views of the horse from below. The shorter White Horse Farm walk is flatter and easier underfoot. The slightly longer Bratton Church walk has quite a steep descent and ascent but includes a pretty church and woods.

Longer walk 8 miles:

Facing the information boards leave the car park, turning left **[1]** and follow the tarmac road across the hilltop towards Westbury. After about 600 yards, where the road bends right and goes downhill, keep directly ahead along an unmetalled track. The track initially passes a huge chalk quarry on the left **[A]**. *You are on the IRPP and the MWW as well as the WR, for part of the way at least.* Follow the track for 2¼ miles, eventually descending Upton Cow Down to head towards the busy A350.

Turn left at the T-junction onto the slip road to Upton Scudamore **[B]** just before reaching the A350, cross the bridge over it, and walk through the village as far as the Angel Inn. Take the byway to the right of the inn, which passes to the right of the telephone and post boxes. This leads down to the Upton Scudamore Water Treatment Plant. Go past the entrance to the Plant buildings, take the footpath on your right which passes between two fences, through a kissing gate and up some wooden steps to a gate into a large field. Go straight across this, passing very close to a telegraph pole. Bear left at a hedge corner and follow the obvious path through a hedge and onto a farm track. Turn right down this to arrive at the road through Old Dilton **[C]**.

Turn left and follow this road through Old Dilton. In 150 yards, just before the bridge over Biss Brook, and St Mary's church, turn right to follow a signposted footpath. Cross two fields going through kissing gates, keeping to the left-hand field edge, then exit through a further kissing gate to reach Dilton Vale Farm. Turn right at the permissive path and follow it round the edge of the farm – this is well signposted. Cross the bridge over the stream and immediately turn right to re-cross it, then ignore the stile ahead of you and cross the stream once again on the right and go through the kissing gate. Turn left and head uphill to a field gate at the top and pass through. Head across this field for 75 yards keeping the hedge on your right and go through a kissing gate in the hedge on the right. Continue along an initially narrow, enclosed footpath (barbed wire fence on the right, care required) for

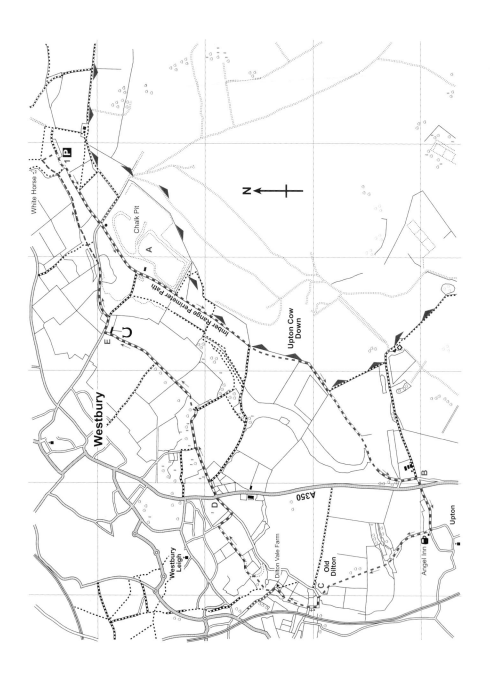

350 yards to a junction on the edge of Westbury Leigh. Turn right along a track and after 150 yards, left along a lane to reach the A350.

Cross the main road **[D]** into Wellhead Drove and follow the lane for ½ mile, passing a number of large houses, until you reach a water board installation. Follow the track to the left of the building for just over ½ mile to the road by the White Horse Equestrian Centre **[E]**. *Here you have your first view of the Westbury White Horse.* Turn right and follow the road uphill for ½ mile to a kissing gate on the left. Go through the gate and walk towards a rusty metal tank ahead, next to which is an abandoned Jack Dean Oils tanker. Continue beside the fence on the left across two fields back towards the White Horse. Beyond the kissing gate in the corner of the second field, follow the path up through some scrubland to a topograph, indicating the direction and distance of notable landscape features and the White Horse. *You may be lucky enough to see paragliders or hang-gliders here. There are a number of benches affording wonderful views stretching many miles.* Turn right across the hilltop to return to the car park **[1]**.

Shorter walks:
Both start by the information boards **[1]**. Map on page 28.

Cross the road, go through the gate and walk straight on to the edge of the escarpment where there are three benches **[2]**. *The White Horse is clearly visible to your right and there are fine views here over the vale below.*

Go down the steps and through the gate to the right and follow the path as far as the ear of the White Horse **[4]** on your left.

At this point, go down steps to your right and up steps to the inner rampart of Bratton Camp **[3]** an Iron Age hill fort. Turn left and follow the rampart round to the right until you see a stile onto the road **[5]**. Do not go over this stile but go to the left of it, through a broken gate and walk downhill parallel to the road. Near the bottom you will see a field gate, do not go through this but veer slightly left still going downhill until you come to a gate onto the road **[6]**.

Turn right up the road. Almost immediately you will see a path leading off at an angle to the left. Follow this and ignore the stile on the right **[7]**, which would take you up between the embankments and back to the car park. Continue up the path until you come to a field gate with a smaller gate up a bank on the left **[8]**.

Map for Shorter Walks

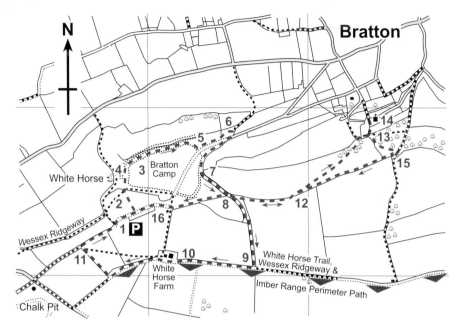

From here you now have the choice of a fairly flat walk of 2½ miles *(page 28)* **or a hillier walk of 3 miles** *(page 29).*

Fairly flat walk of 2½ miles

Go through the field gate **[8]** (not the small gate up a bank on the left) and uphill between grassy banks. Near the top follow the path round to the left by the fence and then right between two fences.

Go through (or over) two field gates onto a track crossing at right angles **[9]**. Turn right. This is the WHT and the WR.

On the other side of the track is Ministry of Defence land – do not go in there.

Follow this track gently uphill to a group of barns, a water tower and a clump of trees – White Horse Farm **[10]**. Follow the gravel track along the edge of the MOD land, turning right when the track does.

This will bring you to a narrow road **[11]** (going left will take you down into Westbury). Turn right and follow the grassy track which runs parallel to the road and past a beacon. *The beacon was placed here for the Golden Jubilee of Queen Elizabeth II, and resembles the millennium beacons.* Continue along the grassy track back to the car park **[1]**.

Hillier walk of 3 miles:

Go through the small gate up the bank on the left **[8]**, follow the path between fences, through a gate and then follow the top of the combe with the fence on your right. After about 300 yards look out for a small footpath sign on a fence post **[12]** where you will see a grassy path heading downhill at an angle to the left. (You will come back to this point.)

Follow this path downhill aiming for a church tower among the trees. Keep going downhill and then between the lines of old trees to a kissing gate on the right. Go through this into an area of smaller trees then through another kissing gate on the right. When you get to a metal kissing gate **[13]** if you want to explore the church and Bratton continue downhill with the church and churchyard, on your right. As you near the church **[14]** you will hear rushing water and looking to the left may be able to see a small lake. You will have to come back the same way to the metal kissing gate **[13]**.

Go through the gate at **[13]**, bear right and follow a steep path up, always up, through the trees. At the top **[15]** you will reach a signpost and a sunken track, do not go into this but turn right to follow a narrow path up the slope and parallel to the sunken track until you meet the corner of a fence. Keep straight on and follow the path along the top of the slope with the fence on your left and then through a gate.

When you reach the post **[12]** mentioned earlier go straight on and follow the top of the combe through another kissing gate, between fences to the next gate **[8]**. Go through this and straight on over a stile then uphill with the fence on your left until you reach another stile onto the road to the car park. Cross the road.

If you look slightly to your left you will see a large stone **[16]** *which commemorates the Battle of Ethandun fought in May 878AD.* Follow the path to it, then continue back to the car park **[1]**.

Westbury White Horse & Bratton Camp

29

Disclaimer

Every effort has been made to ensure the accuracy of the information contained in this book. The Mid-Wilts Group of the Ramblers cannot accept any responsibility for errors, omissions or changes outside their control, which affect the accuracy of the routes described in the text; or for the consequences arising.

Problems on Paths

If you find any problems such as damaged stiles, missing signposts, crops growing over paths or fallen trees, please report them at:

www.my.wiltshire.gov.uk/public-right-of-way

or using the Ramblers Pathwatch app

The postal address is:

The Rights of Way Section
Wiltshire Council, Bythesea Road,
Trowbridge, Wiltshire, BA14 8JN

Also published by Mid-Wilts Ramblers:
Ten Walks around Devizes

Wiltshire White Horse Trail

A 90 mile continuous walk linking all the White Horses, and other historic and prehistoric locations, created by Wiltshire Ramblers in conjunction with Wiltshire Tourism. A detailed route description in both directions has been prepared by Tim Lewis and is available as two free downloads which can be found on the Long Distance Walkers Association website (ldwa.org.uk).

The Mid-Wilts Group

The Mid-Wilts Group of The Ramblers is centred on Devizes and walks regularly in the area.

Abbreviations are used in the text for the various long distance and named paths: Imber Range Perimeter Path (IRPP), Mid-Wilts Way (MWW), Pewsey Avon Trail (PAT), Tan Hill Way (THW), The Ridgeway (TR), Wansdyke Path (WP), Wessex Ridgeway (WR), and White Horse Trail (WHT)

All rights reserved

Printed on paper produced from sustainable forests.